MARRIAGE PRINCIPLES FOR COUPLES

Brenda D. Morin

CONTENTS

Introduction

Recognizing The Meaning Of "Marriage"

- *The definition of the term "Marriage," which has been in use for millennia, has changed with time. Originally, it referred to a merger of two families. Originally, it could only apply to a union of one man and one woman, but it is now open to all forms of partnerships.*

- *Marriage is an emotional bond and a commitment to share a life together.*

- *The social institution of marriage is one that is often taken for granted. It is a custom that has been followed for many years and is still widely used in modern culture.*

- *The union of two individuals who love each other is a common definition of marriage, but it does not include all of its complexities. Marriage may be seen as a social contract between two people, a*

commitment to cohabit, share their lives, and look out for one another until death.

- *Marriage is seen in various faiths as the uniting of one man and one woman. A compact between two individuals who love one another is a relatively recent definition of marriage.*

- *Marriage is a lifetime commitment that offers security, stability, and companionship, whether it is the result of a contract or love.*

When you take into account the ups and downs of daily living, marriage may be both beautiful and difficult. My hubby and I have experienced numerous difficulties together throughout the years. We have created a fulfilling existence that is anything from typical, despite strife in the family and financial hardships. The highs and lows of daily living over time came to characterize our partnership. We started to view marriage as a chance to confront challenging circumstances with bravery and optimism, even when it seemed like everything was going wrong. Our marriage got stronger as we realized how crucial it is to rely on one another through trying times. More than ever before, we were able to feel love, closeness, and delight. We developed into people who are able to deal with the outside world in a calm manner. We improved as humans as a result of our marriage.

While culture differs from nation to nation, marriage is a custom that is accepted all around the globe. It may be seen in religious rites and celebrations, including Christian and Hindu weddings. Marriage has traditionally played a significant role in society in many nations. However, contemporary civilization has advanced recently with many people considering alternate lifestyles for people that allow for many kinds of partnerships. Domestic partnerships, polyamorous relationships, and same-sex marriage are a few of them. The social institution of marriage is one that is often taken for granted. It is a custom that has been followed for many years and is still widely used in modern culture. While culture differs from nation to nation, marriage is a custom that is accepted all around the globe.

Matrimony is another word for marriage. A wedding is the usual ceremony that is carried out when two individuals are married. There are many motives for getting married. It has a legal component. Additionally, it has a social and emotional component. It is also regarded as being cost-effective. And maybe most significantly, it has spirituality and religion at its core.

Despite the fact that some weddings are planned, some individuals see marriage as the beginning of family life and reproduction. The family unit as a legal structure and the legal protection of children come under the hierarchy, which is headed by marriage. Marriage is also seen as a publicly acknowledged commitment. Even though marriage is a widespread custom around the globe, every culture still has its own customs. Marriage is

complicated in that two individuals are legally and financially obligated to one another.

Relationships, which are ultimately a link between two individuals, are where marriage finds its essence. Relationships may be platonic or passionate in nature. But in a marriage, connections are based on transparency and trust. The connection between the husband and wife has to be solid and steady, especially considering how many concessions and efforts marriage includes. In traditional families, the woman is seen as the matriarch and the husband as the provider for the home and the children. The jobs aren't as clearly defined as they once were, however, because of how times have evolved.

Today, some dads who remain at home take care of the household's requirements as well as those of the kids. On the other side, some spouses work 9 to 5 jobs and are the only ones responsible for paying the bills. Women's empowerment has increased, which has led to an increase in their desire to be independent in all senses of the term. Some men have come to the realization that they like having children and playing the mother. However, marriage and relationships go hand in hand. Due to the fact that both the husband and wife are now in charge of one another, it is really a juggling act.

The everyday grind and emotional demands of each person provide challenges in marriage and relationships. The obligation to earn enough money to support the family exists. However, there is also a need for one

another to provide emotional stability. The institution of marriage has, regrettably, become contaminated and ruined. Some unions are just for financial gain. Others occur as a result of parent-arranged marriages. Additionally, there are others who are interested in obtaining citizenship. Marriage and relationships are complicated and multifaceted, yet they have a long history and are still developing today.

Everywhere in the globe, there are married individuals who want a more contented, joyful marriage. They are found all throughout. No matter where you travel, you will encounter them. Most likely, you fall into that category.

So why don't people have better marriages if there are individuals around who want them?
Surely, getting married the way one wishes to can't be that difficult.

Why don't individuals have the marital relationships they desire? People don't often have the sort of marital relationships they want because they don't want to put out any effort to be likable, appealing, beautiful, or seductive.

Their worldview may be summed up as "You should simply adore me as I am for who I am without any effort, cooperation, collaboration, contribution, compromise, or change from me," and if they could only find a way to convince their partner to share it, they would be overjoyed.

However, it is obvious that this is a biased standard since they undoubtedly do not love their spouse for who they are in their current state.

They want unrestricted, unqualified, and undeserved love, yet they have no desire to show it to anybody. They would tell you a lengthy list of modifications, upgrades, and additions your partner would need to do before they could love them and be content with them if you gave them a chance.

- The basic line, my friend, is that you are a worthwhile human being with a lot of potential, and the fact that God created you and placed you on this planet proves that. You are not lovable, attractive, desirable, or sexy to your spouse just because you are here taking up space, and your spouse is not lovable, attractive, desirable, or sexy to you just because they happen to be in your life, despite how much you might want it to be the case and how idyllic it might sound.

Nobody is drawn to a slop or a blob, and nobody wants someone with a soured, negative, angry, bitter, or unpleasant attitude, regardless of who you are or who you believe you are. It takes work, cooperation, collaboration, participation, compromise, and change from you to be loving, appealing, desired, and seductive. The same applies to your spouse as well. If you want to be wanted and valued, you must be and do certain things.

- The second factor preventing people from having the kind of marriage relationship they desire is the way they minimize the needs, wants, and desires of their spouse as being superficial, silly, unimportant, and unnecessary.

While the wife is aware of the husband's aspirations, she does not feel it is necessary for her to fulfill them. Because these are not something he wants, when a woman shares her wishes to her husband, he ignores them.

What you need to realize is that you are actively contributing to an unhappy marriage if your spouse has a need and you expect they should just be fine without you providing that need.

- The third factor that prevents individuals from having the sort of marital connection they want is the bad feelings they retain against their partner. Focusing on previous wrongdoings and complaints gives them a peculiar sense of pleasure and strange emotional stimulation, but ultimately leads to an unhappy self and an unhappy marriage.

Many individuals are also quite skilled at looking forward into the future and conjuring up new grievances and transgressions against their partner in order to feel even worse about themselves and their marriage.

People that are happily married discover and concentrate on the current positive qualities in their spouse.

- Ignorance is the fourth reason individuals don't have the sort of marital connection they desire. They never figured out how to communicate with their partner in a manner that benefits them both. They have never been taught how to communicate with their partner in a manner that fosters mutual harmony, pleasure, fulfillment, and happiness. Men and women are not the same. They vary from one another in how they think, act, and function. As a result, they cannot communicate with one another. And since they cannot communicate with one another, disputes and transgressions often arise.

As a consequence, they are trapped in an unhappy marriage with a partner whom they do, on some level, love but with whom they are just not content. They don't feel content with their partner despite wanting to.

Ignorance is not bliss, as you can surely confirm from your own marriage, my friend. Your lack of comprehension does not result in happiness for you. Until you educate yourself and come to understand your spouse's way of thinking, acting, and operating, you cannot have a happy, fulfilling, and fulfilling marriage. You cannot have a loving, affectionate, and intimate relationship.

50 years ago, you and your spouse could bumble along for 10 to 20 years before coming to a conclusion on your own. You don't have to put up with unhappiness, though, because in today's society, the mentality is "Just get a divorce, find someone else, and start over."

As a result, you only have a few years at most to figure out and perfect your marriage relationship before your spouse decides to get a divorce or have an affair instead of you. Don't you think that learning about yourself is much less expensive and much more enjoyable than dealing with a divorce or an affair?

You must now make a personal decision as you think about your marriage. Some individuals may conclude that it is simpler and more comfortable to just accuse and criticize their spouse for all of their problems. These are the couples whose marriage will deteriorate over time until it finally dissolves.

These are the people who choose to feel unhappiness more and more, which makes their spouse feel even more distant. They are often ready and prepared to start learning what they need to have learnt much earlier when their marriage begins to deteriorate and marital collapse seems inevitable. Of course, it's often too late at this point. But each person is free to use their own judgment and reap the benefits of those decisions.

The good news is that you now have the chance to learn how to build an intimate marriage connection with your spouse that is joyful, loving, and caring so that you never have to struggle with a divorce or extramarital affairs. Don't let this chance pass you by or be wasted.

Chapter 1

The Concept of Marriage

The first premise is monogamy. This indicates that one individual should only have one spouse at any one time. The second concept is sexual faithfulness, which is to be sexually exclusive with one person at any one moment. The third principle is permanency, which indicates that marriage should remain for life or until death does your part. The fourth concept is mutual loyalty which implies having loyalty to your partner no matter what occurs and never giving up on them no matter how bad things become. The fifth premise is equality,

Marriage is a solemn bond between two people who love each other and wish to spend their lives together.

Most marriages often start with "a boy meets a girl" narrative that blossoms into a particular partnership united by love, dedication, and trust that appears to be never-ending. That lovely bond is finally cemented in a ritual

of marriage by a pledge of faithfulness and love for one other and only death can split them apart.

Generally, individuals opt to marry because of Adoration and the pleasure and satisfaction it offers. Others opt into marriage for convenience; friendship or security reasons while other persons follow the instructions of the Bible. There are also a few individuals who cave in to the demands of family and society that's why they marry.

A good marriage is distinctive to every pair. There is no model for an ideal marriage. Finding the proper partner who shares your notion of an ideal and pleasant married life is the key to it. Between you and your spouse, there should be love, trust, respect, open discussions, honesty, humility, gratitude and a good sense of humor, sharing of responsibilities, and ultimate commitment and faithfulness.

A marriage will succeed when there is no pride for both you and your spouse and when you can still admire each other even through times of difficulty or when things don't turn out correctly. You must know how to acknowledge both your errors and be ready to forgive. Learn to compromise.

Another aspect that might help your marriage click is to become each other's closest buddy. You must have same aims and ambitions like a team and you should have respect for each other's families. Most of all, keeping the relationship strong, spending time together, and having wonderful sex may undoubtedly make your marriage better and more interesting.

We all understand by now that not all marriages are a bed of roses. Some have been challenging but couples managed to preserve them. Unfortunately, others ended up in divorce.

Trying to make a marriage work is a collaborative effort by the partners and it needs work. Communication has a critical element in sustaining a happy marriage. Couples should be able to address topics facing their relationship, including children, job, sex, or even home management. What is vital is that couples should spend quality time together despite busy schedules and do something together that they both like.

Whatever your motives or purpose for getting married, don't forget that the basic foundation that will make it work is the love that you both had from the moment you two met and set plans of sharing your life together forever as husband and wife. So, don't let that love go away!

All married couples dispute at one point or another. Remember this guideline for fighting fair which states sentiments are neither good nor evil, they only are. Accept your spouse's sentiments even if you don't share them. Arguing over who's right frequently leads to animosity. You may be correct is a helpful saying in which the speaker doesn't concede to being wrong, but acknowledges your partner has a legitimate perspective. Occasionally that's enough to break a stalemate.

In a debate, we lead and follow. It's like a dance in which we have to be alert to the signals of the other and balance our own demands with those of our partner. Are you more of a leader or a follower? A good argument may be a labor of love. Have anything sensitive or tough to speak about with your spouse? Try holding hands and keeping direct eye contact while you are addressing a dispute.

When you and your partner disagree over anything, consider shifting places symbolically. Take your spouse's stance to experience how it feels from another point of view. You don't have to agree, but it helps your partner to know you understand. It may minimize repetition and screaming. Share your emotions without resentment. It requires awareness to detect when your partner is struggling. What appears like fury could be fear or hurt.

"I think you were correct." Although marriage is not a competition, nonetheless this sentence is one of the loveliest things a spouse can say. It may arise after a conflict in which both parties were confident they were correct. It doesn't solve the error but it's so much better than "I told you so!" Is there anything your husband was correct about recently?

Lastly, don't argue with anybody today even if you're correct. And if someone has to win an argument, let it be your husband. Even if you argue, don't make your spouse incorrect. You don't have to win every dispute, otherwise you forfeit the marriage.

Chapter 2

Is "HE" the ideal match for me?

Finding the solution to this question is not always simple. Sometimes it's difficult for individuals to realize their partner's potential. They can also be in denial and unwilling to acknowledge the fact that they are unhappy with their spouse.

It is challenging to respond to this question since it requires a thorough examination of both spouses. It's crucial to take into account the character features and values of the potential spouse. ***The first thing you should do is take some time to sit down and identify your values and life goals.*** This will enable you to decide what kind of individual will suit you the most.

Also, make a list of these serious inquiries that you should ask yourself. The first one to ask yourself is, "Do I feel good about him?" Someone is probably the correct one for you if you feel your best with them. Do I want to speak about him all the time? is the second question. You may know your

companion is the one for you if you are always gushing about how wonderful he or she is. Am I interested in what he has to say? is the third question. It's usually a hint that this individual is suitable for you if they give you the impression that they are interested in what's going on in your life and vice versa. Just because you two are together doesn't mean you have to get married. ***Not every relationship results in marriage, or even starts with marriage.***

For a variety of diverse causes, people assemble. Some of those motives are quite selfish and quickly end the relationship. Other explanations may appear to be going well at first, but the relationship ultimately fails and cannot be rescued. It doesn't follow that individuals should get married just because they finally discover the person to whom they can imagine themselves saying "I do."

Marriage is not right for everyone. You are not alone if you are in a relationship and wonder whether he is the one. It's a perennial query that is still challenging to resolve.

But before you make the decision to walk down the aisle, we've put up a list of traits to look for in your partner. In the end, all that matters is whether you want to wed this particular man. Being honest with oneself might be difficult at times.

Is he actually the one? Here are 15 indications that he may be:

1. You're not only there for the sex.

Every relationship begins steamy and passionate, and you find it difficult to keep your hands off of one another. You spend every free moment in the bedroom. But it is short-lived. Every relationship passes through many phases of intimacy, and with time, partners transition from the lust-filled stage to the companion stage. You need to think about if your companionship will alter with time, even while your sexual attraction to this individual may vary.

Are you only there for the sex? Could this be a factor in the fact that you keep thinking about him?

Are you not considering a long-term connection with this individual, but only hoping to get something from them?

While being attracted to your spouse is crucial, you also need to be able to handle how your attraction to them varies over time. People's appearances fluctuate. In thirty years, how will you feel about them?

2. You get along.

Your perspective on attraction as well as your compatibility with this individual should be taken into account. You can't have a long-lasting relationship if the only thing you like doing together is having wonderful sex.

How about him? Here are the key details that you need to be aware of.

Do you have a similar taste in at least some things?

Are the meals you like the same?

Can you both watch the same movies?

Are you able to communicate well with your pals and exchange stories?

A successful marriage is not likely to result from a lack of compatibility outside of the bedroom. Think about how you want your daily life to be. Is this the individual who can assist in bringing that life to you?

3. You feel at ease in his presence.

How at ease do you feel with him? Do you still withhold information from him and refuse to let him in on some aspects of your life? Is he acting in the same way?

You are not prepared to be married if you hold back on sharing details of your life out of concern that he will judge you or, worse yet, abandon you. But if you know you can be true to yourself no matter what, and he doesn't hold you accountable for past mistakes, **then he's definitely a good partner for marriage.**

He is aware of your history, but is just considering the future? **Save him.**

Observing how he behaves under pressure is another excellent indicator of if he is the one. Is he trying to keep you safe? Or does he simply consider himself?

4. Respect exists between the two of you.

Every partnership requires respect and affection. Despite what you would believe, many individuals profess to love others while treating them with disrespect. You understand what we're talking about if you've ever met someone whose spouse has mistreated them despite their strong belief that they are loved.

For a marriage to succeed, love and respect must always coexist and not be mutually incompatible.

5. You're free with his relatives.

If you're debating whether you should marry this guy, think about how you would get along with his relatives and how you would respect and understand his past.

There will be issues if you don't get along with his family in the future. It could be okay right now since you are handling it, but do you want to commit to something that will bring you stress in the future?

It's worth thinking about or contemplating getting married if you already have a difficult relationship with his family. Taking a commitment does not automatically make anything easier.

6. You both anticipate a similar future together.

You acknowledge one another in the future when you discuss it. If you can picture a future with him, that's terrific, but if he never discusses such things with you, *it may not be the perfect match.*

7. You consent to being at odds

To marry this man, you don't always have to get along with him. In fact, it's preferable if you don't always agree. Your partnership is solid because you both understand that you may have opinions on things that are different from his.

It's a good indicator not to get married if you are made to feel uneasy because your opinions differ from his. Since you are meant to complement one another in life, you are not meant to be the same person. However, being complimentary does not obligate you to constantly concur with him. He deserves your hand if you are content with not sharing your viewpoint on every subject.

8. You respect each other's individuality.

Even if you two are in love, you accept that you are two separate people with lives that existed before you met. This implies that you have a career, friends, and family who sometimes need you and who need you in return.

Even if you may have discovered each other, you still sometimes need to be apart. He's a fantastic companion if he allows you enough of space to continue living your life but yet wanting to be involved.

Run as far away from him as you can if he asks you to give up all you know and love in order to be with him alone.

9. He keeps you safe.

A decent man will constantly ensure that his spouse feels secure, both physically and emotionally. Does your man protects you? Not only does he

protect you from physical injury, but does he also check on you in case something bad happens?

This is a strong indication that he could be the one. An interesting new idea in relationship psychology is now generating a lot of excitement. It answers the fundamental question of why men fall in love and with whom they fall in love. And that completely explains why males desire to defend women. And the reason why women must condone this conduct. Because you must give him permission if he wants to protect you.

For the lady in their life, men want to step up and take responsibility for her care and protection. To put it another way, guys want to be your hero. This is built into a man's mentality and firmly ingrained in his genetics. The worst part is that if a guy doesn't feel like your hero, he won't fall in love with you. He won't make the long-term commitment to being in a loving relationship since he will always feel as if something is lacking.

10.   You interact more deeply.

It's not only about having fantastic sex together; it's also about connecting in a way that you've never done before. He repeats himself. He feels comfortable with you and confident in you to handle any situation.

It's not a good sign for a marriage if you feel like you are simply a pit stop on his weekend excursions. You should hold onto him if he is attempting to

find out how to spend more time with you and is presentable and responsible while he is there.

11.   You are considerate and polite to one another.

Much more than just liking one another is involved in being in a relationship. Sometimes a couple's love isn't enough to keep them together. The partnership won't be sustained if there is no mutual respect or consideration.

If he treats you badly, it makes no sense to stay in the relationship, even if you love him more than you've ever loved anything. Of course, leaving is difficult, but so is putting up with being mistreated. He's a keeper, however, if he respects and loves you, which are two whole different things.

12.   You help him feel necessary.

Make him feel important to you if he really is the one. Because *like* and *love* may sometimes be distinguished by a man's sense of being indispensable to a woman.

Don't get me wrong; your man undoubtedly admires your fortitude and independence. He still wants to feel needed and valuable rather than disposable, however. Men naturally yearn for something higher than sex or romantic love. It explains why guys who seem to have the ideal relationship

nonetheless struggle with loneliness and find themselves looking for new things or, worse still, new people all the time.

Simply said, males have a biological urge to support the woman they care about and to feel wanted and valued.

13. You sense that he can be authentic.

You don't have to keep everything from him, but if there are aspects of your life that you'd prefer keep under lock and key, he respects your limits. He constantly expresses his appreciation for being able to be himself with you. In this connection, you understand each other and what you both require.

He could be the one if you feel free to be who you are with him, even on your worst hair days, and there is no pressure to change who you are.

14. You feel secure around him.

He gives you the confidence to take on the world. He behaves properly, but not in the same way that the rest of the world does or that you would want to be treated. He is pleased to take care of your requirements since he is aware of them. He's not trying to change who you are to fit his needs.

He's worth marrying if you can be authentic and don't feel the need to put on a show for him. He has saw you at your worst and yet loved you. Such is love. And marriage is all about it.

15. You want him to rejoice.

Most significantly, your desire for his happiness is the greatest indication that you should wed this man. Although the thought of him being married to someone else makes your heart hurt, you would support it if it would make him happy. Tell him that you naturally want him to love his life with you and be happy with you.

Tell him that you want him to have a happy life and that you want to be the one to share it with. There's no reason to keep your emotions hidden. Go for it if you want to wed him.

Chapter 3

Understanding the Power of Jealousy

We tend to blame ourselves for having envy, but it's important to remember that it's a normal human feeling that we're all born with. You should learn to comprehend it so that you may change, not be embarrassed to experience it.

Try to look at other women as inspiration rather than as rivals. Reframe your mindset to be "If she can accomplish it, so can I" rather than "What does this person have that I don't?" Try to follow women on social media, for instance, who inspire and make you feel represented. On social media, unfollow ladies whose posts make you feel horrible. Put your inner tranquility first.

"At first, I wasn't conscious of what others were saying behind my back, but soon enough, the downhill spiral started. However, I had the ability to influence events in my favor, and I did so with optimism.

Try not to allow it to adversely alter your view when someone at work or university has what you don't. Instead, make an effort to comprehend the cause of your feelings. Try to identify where that feeling came from.

Then, by being conscious of what you have, turn the sensation of envy into something positive. Every person has a certain path and calling. Someone may be better than you at something, own something you do not currently possess, or be at a different stage than you.

Try to be pleased for other ladies rather than being envious of them. "That's terrific for her, but I'm fine and pleased with who and where I am right now," say to yourself. At least one of our friends always performs better than we do. Although it may be difficult at first, try to be really pleased for your pals. Allow your buddies to motivate you to improve.

The best course of action is to isolate yourself from them if you continue to experience envy. Spend some time focusing on who you are and what you want to achieve. The envious sentiments will soon go away and be replaced with feelings of confidence. But in order to safeguard your mental health and prevent animosity in your friendship, you must temporarily distance yourself from them.

You'll seldom ever understand why someone seems unusual to you. You don't need to spend time overthinking your previous deeds. It is not up to

you to worry about why someone is behaving strangely toward you since you may never find out!

Everyone has their own pathways and calling, as was previously said, and you are no exception. People may sometimes start to pose a danger to you when they see that you have something they don't because they don't want you to advance.

Nobody's jealousy of you has to be internalized; that's a feeling they have to deal with on their own. Instead, keep your distance, as you would with anybody. Try not to anticipate envy from strangers. Just be conscious of the individuals you draw. Every scenario ought to serve as a teaching opportunity for you.

When dealing with a scenario you are acquainted with, consider if you formerly had a friendship with the person you are drawn to. If so, take a moment to reflect and adjust your relationship in light of the lessons you've gained from previous experiences. Be mindful of your gut instinct. Focus on hearing and believing your inner voice. Before you even consciously consider whether it is a good or terrible circumstance, it will direct you.

Overall, stop feeling envious of others by being really kind to them. The energy you emit into the universe returns to you. You will only draw the best for yourself if you want the best for other people.

Being "green with envy" or having the "green-eyed monster bite you" are two common expressions for jealousy. When the renowned author employs these expressions to characterize a character in The Merchant of Venice, it all dates back to Shakespearian times.

In certain cases, the sensation of envy is a symptom of a psychiatric issue. As a result, both men and women are equally affected by this emotional response. Some claim that a little amount of envy is healthy since it motivates people to improve themselves and aim higher.

Unfortunately, there may be serious repercussions if this illness develops into an obsessive one. Because one spouse felt envious of the other, many partnerships have ended. When you're in love, it's okay to feel a little jealous, but too much might make someone want to leave you.

Why Do People Get Jealous?

Possessions may serve as powerful motivators. You could purchase new clothing and feel motivated to work more if you believe your look falls short of that of a colleague. The emotional response that is associated with jealousy might motivate you to become more active at work or in a relationship and to outperform your rival.

According to several studies, a happy marriage is one where one or both partners exhibit some jealous behavior. Naturally, they have reasonable boundaries and don't go too far into obsession. Between being envious and getting obsessive, there is a thin line.

Being in love with someone may easily be mistaken with being enamored with them and trying to control everything they do. When someone exhibits such habits, the other person feels more like an object than a fellow human being.

An action that is intended to draw someone closer to you may instead suffocate them and push them into the arms of another person. It seems sense that science would characterize jealousy as a complicated emotion with sensations ranging from dread of abandonment to indignant wrath.

Many believe that anxieties on the side of both parties are what lead to mistrust in a relationship. Because you were cheated on in the past, you can lack confidence. Or maybe your significant other's actions have made you feel untrustworthy.

You need to learn to let go of the idea that you have a right to your partner. You cannot take actions to keep them out of your life since they don't belong to you. Because they believe their spouse is more appealing than they deserve, one partner in a relationship may sometimes develop jealousy. To attempt to keep this individual around, they could act out or say things that are motivated by internal fears. In this circumstance, the individual who feels inferior to others may exhibit suspicious behavior and obsession.

The primary causes of envy in every relationship stem from your own self-doubt and insecurities. These are the main causes of this emotional response, thus.

Five (5) Main Reasons for Jealousy

- Issues with one's self-image

- Negative encounters in previous partnerships

- Fear of being left behind

- Anxiety problems

- Due to personality features, more likely to experience these emotions

Scientists have classified three different types of jealousy since it is such a significant problem. The categories are as follows:

- **Reactive** (acting in reaction to a situation rather than creating or directing it)

Someone who envies the reactive group has good grounds for their problems. For instance, if your partner has betrayed you in the past,

whether once or many times, your jealousy may be fueled by your declining level of confidence in them.

- **Suspicious** (having or expressing a careful skepticism of someone or something)

Some couples have a tendency to flirt a little. Even while you may not be aware of any specific interactions between your husband and anybody else, you could be skeptical of this flirting. Many times, there is nothing going on between the other two persons, and the problem is being caused by your fears.

- **Pathological** (involving or caused by a bodily or mental ailment) (involving or caused by a physical or mental disease)

It's unhealthy to have a pathological jealousy issue. This individual is someone who lets their bad ideas and delusions rule their thinking. This kind of envious individual may act violently owing to their illogical tendencies. All facets of their lives will be impacted by their mistrust problems, which may also have an impact on their health. They may experience anxiety and high blood pressure, and their delusions may drive them to the verge of insanity.

Why is Obsessive Jealousy Risky?

Any jealous problem has internal distrust at its core. Obsessive thoughts might arise for the simplest of causes. Consider a scenario when one spouse works longer than usual because of a meeting.

The spouse can be busy working at the workplace. However, if your spouse leaves you home alone for a long period of time, your mind could start to harbor doubts and replay unpleasant memories.

If you struggle with mistrust, you can start to suspect your spouse of cheating if they are working late. You could begin to accept these notions as true when they begin to dominate your thinking, even though you lack any supporting evidence.

You could act and think differently toward them after hours of thought and uncertainty regarding their location. You will believe all of these unfounded possibilities that your mind concocted. Admitting that you have a problem with your jealous nature is the first step towards obtaining treatment.

Did you realize that your tendency to be envious may run in your family? It's true that if your parents had a really jealous mentality, they could have passed those qualities on to you. The most frequent cause of your distrustful attitude, however, is that events in your life have had a negative impact on you. According to the mental health community, someone who is envious is motivated by a lack of self-confidence. Whatever the problem's root source, it's comforting to know that it can be fixed. You must acknowledge that you have envy and be willing to seek treatment.

To prevent your jealousy from damaging what may otherwise be a positive relationship, you must learn how to manage it. Here are the essentials for solving this problem:

1. Determine the Source.

You need to figure out what makes you so suspicious of your spouse, as was already indicated. Do you distrust others in general or do you have poor self-esteem or a sense that you are inferior to others? These underlying problems make you vulnerable, which fuels your fear of being left behind.

Making a list of the issues in your relationship that worry you may be useful. Remember to keep your imagination apart from reality. Knowing what is motivated by fear and what is motivated by action is crucial.

2. Increase Your Self-Belief

Even when someone makes you feel inferior to them, you must never forget your own value. You should never make comparisons to other people because you are excellent on your own terms. Make a list of all your qualities if you notice that you are always comparing yourself to other people. It's likely that you may learn some very fantastic facts about yourself that you were unaware of. Why not enumerate all the factors that led to your partner's first decision to choose you?

3. Examine previous relationships

The first thing you have to do is assess your prior connections. Were other romances making you envious? Did you notice that you were dealing with the same problems in earlier relationships as you are now?

If you discover that this is a persistent condition, you should seek expert assistance. A jealousy problem seldom goes away on its own and has a tendency to intensify and turn into an obsession. You can get through this issue if you work hard and find a decent therapist.

You must refrain from assigning blame. You must figure out what in your present relationship is causing these sentiments if you previously had no problems with jealousy. It's time to talk openly and honestly with your spouse about the aspects of your union that give you pause.

The last thing to keep in mind while dealing with a jealous temperament is that whatever suspicions or obsessions you have will only grow if you keep repeating them. Stop obsessing about things you can't prove, and stop thinking about things repeatedly that don't exist. If you're determined not to let jealousy destroy your life, you can and will overcome this.

A marriage's long-term and immediate objectives

Relationship objectives are ideas, beliefs, or experiences that should be sought for, as well as basic rules on how to show and accept love in a relationship. You might believe that loving someone or being loved comes naturally to you, but not everyone loves in the same way. Relationship goals can help you learn how you and your partner show one another love. Relationship objectives are instruments that assist your relationship develop rather than a stringent set of rules to be adhered to strictly.

The Importance of Relationship Goals

Relationship objectives will, first and foremost, aid in the growth and improvement of your relationship by giving it a purpose. Why not set goals for your relationship as well? You set goals for everything you do, like wanting to get a certain grade on an exam or want to get a certain job promotion within a certain time frame.

It's simple to forget to maintain your connection after you've been in a relationship for a long time and start taking everything for granted. Given that, it's a turning point for you to improve your marriage. We all understand that sustaining relationships involves effort, but sometimes we may not know where to begin. Setting objectives for your relationships may assist. Furthermore, no matter how many relationship objectives you establish, if one or both of you aren't putting out enough effort to achieve them, it may be time to reexamine your partnership. Partnership objectives are thus crucial in a relationship. Oh, we all know the sensation of being intoxicated by love at the beginning of a relationship, but what happens after things settle down? You'll discover that setting relationship objectives will help you maintain a balanced life.

You need to first understand yourself before you get right into creating complicated lists, charts, and mind maps with your spouse. Think on these

issues: Why do you desire what you want in a relationship? What feelings are connected to these needs, furthermore? Are your desires the result of previous events? Following that, you may sit down and speak with your spouse.

Create measurable, concrete, doable, and realistic relationship objectives, then give them a due date. As an example, imagine breaking the year up into four quarters and setting objectives for each one. You'll be more likely to be proactive about the objective if there is a deadline. If you wish, you may also divide your objectives into weekly, monthly, and annual categories. Make sure to be open with your partner about both separate and shared goals, as well as how you can cooperate to achieve them. Some of your relationship goals may be independent from one another.

Setting relationship objectives is a fantastic idea as long as you don't set too many of them. Avoid taking on more than you can handle; 5 objectives is a manageable quantity. Additionally, it's a good idea to create a process for routinely reviewing your objectives to determine if you are making progress toward them, whether they need to be adjusted, whether new goals should be formed, etc. Last but not least, display your objectives so that you can easily see them. This will serve as a constant reminder for you.

Long-Term Goals for Relationships

Long-term relationship objectives, on the other hand, call for more work, time, commitment, and sometimes financial resources to be successful. Usually, a number of short-term objectives are established and completed before attempting to reach a long-term objective. Long-term relationship objectives are still essential to partnerships, even if they can't be achieved quickly, particularly if you and your spouse are in it for the long run.

1. Planning your family

Do you wish to adopt or raise your children? What number do you need? How soon do you need them? In order to avoid a passionate night turning into a life you're both not yet ready to be responsible for, it's essential to address all of these issues as soon as you decide to engage in physical contact. Even if you don't want children at all, you will need to take the necessary precautions to avoid unintended pregnancies, and you both need to be certain about this. Family planning is very important.

2. Purchase a Home

You already know that real estate is often not inexpensive, and purchasing real estate jointly shows that you two are willing to share this load going forward. It might be your residence or a property for investment reasons. Whichever it is, if you decide to live together in a house that you built, purchasing a property is one of your long-term relationship objectives.

3. Get hitched

Additionally, this sounds like a no-brainer, am I right? Even though marriage is the social norm nowadays, not everyone may wish to be married. Your wedding is a long-term relationship objective that you will both look forward to realizing, should you both want to be married to each other! What kind of wedding are you looking for? DJ or band? Simple or opulent? Outside or inside? There are so many choices to make!

4. Create a long-term financial strategy

Although this has been discussed as a short-term relationship objective, you still need a long-term financial strategy. You must carefully evaluate your money if you want to get married, buy a home, have children, five pets, and have it all so that you may live comfortably. When should you have money before getting married? What is the price of the property you are interested in? What will it cost you to raise a child?

5. Talk About The Kids

Then there is, of course, the perennial concern of all parents: their kids. Which teachings and values from your own and your partner's upbringing do you wish to instill in your children? Do you share a few fundamental principles? Which way do you wish to raise your kids? Which institution should they attend? How much should you discipline your kids? These aren't queries that have a one-word solution.

6. **Keep lines of communication open and be affectionate**

Perhaps you believe that you will always express your love for your lover, but it does happen sometimes. Life just takes over, and your relationship somehow suffers as a result of job, children, extreme weariness, or anything else. But keep in mind that you always have your spouse to speak to, and you must keep the lines of communication open, particularly when it comes to issues that are bothering you. Keep it up, guys—even the little actions, like holding hands in the mall, matter!

Short Term Goals for Relationships

A short-term relationship objective is often one that you can complete in less than a year. It is possible to do it now, tomorrow, next week, or in a few months... Providing it doesn't take a year or more. Many individuals have a propensity to jump forward to long-term objectives without appreciating the importance of short-term goals. How can you accomplish a long-term objective if you can't even accomplish a short-term one? To get you started, consider the following examples of short-term relationship objectives.

1. Continue to Be Healthy

Except for athletic couples, some individuals have a tendency to loosen up after they've started dating. Yes, we all have acquaintances that fit that description. However, maintaining good health and fitness is crucial for more reasons than just appearance. You may commit to weekly gym sessions, a yearly marathon, and twice-weekly home-cooked dinners. Together, you should both be in good health!

2. Create a long-term financial strategy

This kind of financial plan is more focused on short-term goals, such as how much you should be saving each month, how much you should budget for food the next month, or how much you'll need for a trip. Nothing major like paying off a vehicle loan or house, so it's absolutely a feasible objective.

3. Maintain Your Wonder

While spending some alone time with your spouse is fine, it's equally crucial to continue learning and experiencing new things so that you will never stop being in awe of one another. There's always the option of taking up a new pastime together, like dance, photography, arts and crafts, or a sport! Simply make sure you do it often, like once a week. Okay, if you're the very busy kind, once a month will do.

4. Increase religious fervour

Perhaps you could develop a regimen for the religious, whether it be attending church each week, going to the temple on Wesak Day, or any other arrangement in between. Given that Christians see God as the supreme being, a relationship based on him ought to be the foundational one. If you and your partner practice different religions, have an open mind as you approach and educate one another about your respective faiths.

5. Show Mutual Interest in One Another's Goals

Although it may not seem like it, something has to be spoken. Sometimes we might get so preoccupied with what we are doing right now that we forget our significant other has interests as well. In addition, a partner's interests may shift from time to time, so it's a good idea to be aware of what fresh item has recently caught their attention. Interests are a terrific subject to discuss and learn more about, whether they change or not, particularly if you're just learning about them now.

How to handle problems that might cause a conflict of interest in a marriage:

There is no ideal marriage without disagreement

In the early stages of a relationship, your companion is the sun rising and setting. But after time, spouses could start to take each other for granted. It's possible that one spouse prefers to spend more time alone or going out with friends. Maybe it drives you mad when you are trying to have a conversation with your spouse and they are scrolling on their phone. When one partner believes that they do not get enough love or care, all these minor fights start.

Remember to express gratitude and show your spouse some love. For your pleasure and the happiness of your marriage, gratitude may go a long way. Planning time to spend with your spouse is essential. You may stay attentive to one another and maintain the romance by scheduling a weekly date night or engaging in another routine activity. The various love languages should also be understood. Even if both couples choose "quality time" as their top love language, each individual may have a different idea of what that means.

- *Sex*

Most marriages only allow you to have sex with your spouse, and some individuals have larger sex desires than others. In a relationship, this may lead to a lot of friction, especially if one person repeatedly wants to initiate sex but is turned down. Don't take your partner's actions too personally and try to have sensible conversations about intimacy. Occasionally, your companion is just worn out.

There may be underlying concerns if one party refuses to engage in sex or is unable to perform. These issues may be resolved through couples counseling, or you can discover another method to probe more than sex to identify the root of the issue.

- *Rivalry and adultery*

A horrible emotion that results from insecurity and/or a lack of trust is jealousy. Couples may feel envious of their spouse when they see them chatting to an ex-girlfriend or ex-boyfriend or flirting with a colleague, but they may also be envious of other things. For instance, if your spouse thinks you have more free time than they do or if you have a pastime you enjoy and they are at home watching it, they can feel envious.

Building or reestablishing trust is often the key to overcoming arguments with jealousy and adultery. If you believe in your spouse, there is no justification for feeling envious of them when they reply to a text from a

former sweetheart or a seductive coworker. Consider enhancing your self-esteem if your jealousy is not connected to (possible) adultery. If you develop a new activity of your own, you won't be as envious of your partner's fascinating new pastime.

- **Duties and obligations**

Arguments about obligations and tasks, which are particularly frequent among parents with small children, may be quite damaging to a marriage. Almost invariably, one partner feels as if they are carrying more of the load.

Establish tasks and responsibilities in advance to prevent this dispute. Even though it seems stupid, a "chore board" may be really helpful. Have the other spouse replace the bedsheets the next weekend if one partner does so one weekend. Alternately, divide the jobs if one partner despises sweeping the floor while the other despises cleaning the bathroom.

The expectations and standards for cleanliness are a major problem when it comes to duties and obligations. For one partner, dirty dishes may not be a huge problem, but they can drive the other spouse insane. Discuss the design of your shared area, determine what needs to be done to make it happen, and divide the labor up among the group.

Remember that you and your spouse may not always be able to do all of your household duties, particularly if one of you is sick or very busy at

work. Ask for assistance when you need it, and provide a hand to your spouse when they want it. When you can afford it, don't be hesitant to hire a babysitter or housekeeper if you and your partner need additional assistance around the home.

- **Dominance and Control**

Although power dynamics have the potential to derail even the strongest of relationships, healthy partnerships are not about dominance and control. You may have heard the comment, "but we always do what you want to do," or one partner may be so possessive as to be out of jealousy.

Consider taking some time apart if you're having a lot of issues with dominance and control. It might seem counterintuitive. Go to the movies by yourself if you don't want to hike with your husband! Make time for the activities you want to do, and while you're with your partner, work out a compromise. If you don't feel like you are abandoning your interests, you will be more ready to compromise. Similar to this, your spouse will be more likely to concur on what you should do with your free time if they have time to follow their hobbies.

You and your spouse will have more to speak about if you pursue acceptable hobbies and activities outside of your marriage, which may help relationships.

- **Future Budget and Plans**

Even the best-laid plans may go awry, so it can be difficult to prepare for the future. In a similar vein, disagreements between spouses about how to manage limited finances may lead to conflict. Parents may disagree on the precise number of field soccer cleats they should get for their children, while newlyweds may disagree about when they want to have a baby.

It takes a lot of effort to share everything and live together forever, but it's worth it. You ought to be able to come up with workable solutions as long as you hold your disagreements in a courteous and healthy manner.

I've devoted the majority of my adult life to studying relationship dynamics: what works, what doesn't, and how we get beyond the pain and into spaces of openness, connection, and love. Even though I consider myself to be a "professional" relationship person, I often find myself and my spouse in awkward circumstances when we both feel misunderstood, ignored, and disrespected. However, this fight was distinct from others in the past because we allowed it to guide us toward, not away from, deeper connections and loving relationships.

Most of us have had disagreements and disputes in our marriages. When we attempt to express our needs or wants to one another, we often feel misunderstood or, worse still, ignored. Our default response is to erupt, remain silent, or give up. But there is an alternative. It doesn't matter if you

and your spouse never argue or have a quarrel; what matters is what you do when one does arise.

- **Following the battle, becoming closer**

We realize that we have misinterpreted one another after the agitated, rising shouts or icy silence. The next course of action offers us the chance to either allow the disagreement drive us apart or bring us closer. We need some fresh skills in our relationship arsenal if we want to become closer via disagreement.

My husband usually appears to be on his phone while we're conversing, which may be frustrating. However, it's not necessarily the phone that's the issue; rather, it's the way I feel ignored whenever I try to contact him.

The bulk of disagreements between partners are caused by differences in our personalities, wiring, or values. When we argue, many of us fail to probe further into the issues that are troubling us and instead focus just on what is in front of us. The next time you and your partner disagree, let curiosity guide you toward identifying the core issue.

Curiosity made me see that when I'm attempting to communicate with my partner but he's scrolling on his phone, I mistakenly assume that he doesn't care about me. That is the main issue. The cellphone comes in second.

We become aware of our true pains, wants, and longings when we are interested about how we see and interpret the world. And from there, closeness may develop.

- **Leaving behind behaviors**

Fighting over actions often prevents us from dealing with more delicate questions of desire and need. But when we're ready to go beyond the habits and into more in-depth dialogues, breakthroughs occur. Then we may be brave and vulnerable enough to share ourselves with one another.

As an example, I once dealt with a couple called Kloe and Davidson who had behavioral problems. They argued over parenting, weekend plans, and date nights with other couples.

Beyond the actions, though, Kloe found Davidson to be unresponsive to her ideas and to react defensively when she attempted to bring them up. When Davidson wanted to "have it out," Kloe would frequently withdraw and become silent. This annoyed Davidson.

They needed to have more in-depth discussions about how their conduct, such quarreling about weekend plans, resulted in emotions of anger and disappointment, and how each person was perceiving those feelings in

order to get beyond these disputes in their marriage. These moments would only occur if Davidson (or Kloe) could frankly state, "I felt irritated that you left when we spoke about weekend plans. That gave me the impression that you were uninterested in or unwilling to spend time with me.

- **Establishing ties via compromise**

Conflict seems most dangerous when we are cut off from one another. Fear and insecurity come to the surface when we dispute and then put space between us. Instead of really resolving the disagreement, we often defend ourselves by accusing, protecting, or consenting. But when we stay connected, we may often make concessions in order to join with love.

When we let down our guard and affirm the other's experience, a deeper connection results. Even while it sometimes happens, this does not always include saying sorry. Validating entails selecting empathy that expresses, "I can see how you might feel that way" or "Now that I hear your side, I can appreciate how it would be challenging, frustrating, disappointing." The ability to go out of our comfort zone and declare, "I'm open to perceiving things differently," is validation.

Communicating commitment is another way we get from defensiveness to connection. Simply stating "I'm on your team" or "I'm dedicated to us and I want to work through this" might convey commitment. When we demonstrate commitment, we allay the other person's worries that a disagreement would cause the relationship to fall apart.

Without connection, making a compromise seems like losing. Consensual compromise evokes feelings of affection. When we make the decision to seek understanding, let go off old habits, and maintain our connection despite disagreement, we experience this form of closeness. One discussion at a time, when we are linked, conflict becomes less frightening and love deepens.

Chapter 4

Friends and Marriage (Social Circles)

Being Married Can Possibly Affects Your Relationship With Friends

It's reasonable to assume that for many of us, marriage is one of the most significant partnerships in our lives. It's a struggle we all confront in life, one that affects relationships with spouses as well as with friends and family. But if you see that your marriage is hurting your relationships, hold off on calling the divorce lawyers! Instead, you must choose how to approach it like you would any other issue.

Let's go through some of the typical worries and disputes that might arise when we get married. It won't be a gloomy grind, so don't worry! Ideally, you'll leave not just with greater knowledge, but also with confidence in the durability of your partnership.

- ### *The issue of having the wrong friends*

You may have observed that you don't socialize with your single pals as much now that you're married. That's fine and totally comprehensible! Although it wouldn't necessarily be accurate to state that they're envious, the fact that you were once single and shared that characteristic with them no longer exists. This might make it challenging to connect to one another since, although their tales of disastrous dinner dates are diverse, yours will almost always feature your spouse.

It might also be unpleasant for your single pals to spend out with you and your significant other since they can feel embarrassed or, worse, like you succeeded in finding love while they haven't. Your partner can object if you go out with your single friends or girlfriends without them since they might think you're attempting to get away from your new life.

How do you approach this? Do you just allow those friendships to go away? Even if it undoubtedly does occur, it is not necessary. You need to find a method to stay connected with them without making your marriage a point of controversy if you want to avoid the third wheel problem or the insecure spouse problem.

I tried to host people more often throughout my marriage. I've organized several dinner gatherings, board game evenings, and movie trips

throughout the years. My husband and I, as a family of faith, have expanded our involvement with our local church, something we first resisted doing but have since discovered to be quite beneficial in helping us maintain our community involvement in interesting and entertaining ways.

• *meeting new people*

Long-term relationships make it more difficult for both of you to establish friends, as anybody who has been in one can attest. Although it's conceivable to keep up your old connections (as was already discussed), there are situations when it's just not feasible. However, as humans are social beings, we all need a social life. How do you make new acquaintances when it becomes tougher as you grow older, is the question.

Do you recall why making friends in high school or college was simpler at that time? It wasn't simply that you met folks with a lot in common by chance. It was because you were compelled to be together, maybe because you had the same courses. That is why you two should think about enrolling in a class, especially one that will teach you both a new skill.

My other acquaintance just got married, and he and his wife had the same issue. Even while they continued to be supportive, over time they found that they have very little in common with their single friends. They could socialize with other couples, but those couples had their own schedules and

obligations. In the end, my buddy and his wife started to experience the stresses of isolation but lacked the social skills to do so.

I saw this and proposed that they enroll in a course together. No matter what sort of lesson they took, if they could study it with a group of individuals who were at a similar ability level, it would foster a feeling of camaraderie that would make friendships easier to develop. Improvement, ballroom dance, and painting were discussed, but they eventually settled on ceramics. They both thought it would be enjoyable even if they had any ceramic abilities.

Indeed, they had gotten along with several of their classmates by the conclusion of the six-week course. They now host their get-togethers with these new acquaintances, when everyone eats dinner, drinks wine, and spends a few hours molding clay.

These are some typical problems that newlywed couples deal with. These problems, as well as many others that a new family can encounter, can all be resolved. Marriage can have an impact on your friendships and familial ties, but it isn't necessarily hopeless, particularly if you know how to manage the changes.

Benefits and Risks of Friendships Outside of Marriage

Having friends is not prohibited if you are married. A lot of instances, marriages bring together groups of friends! Together, your friends and your spouse's friends make up the sizable group known as "our friends." Nevertheless, regardless of how close you may be to other couples, you probably have single acquaintances or pals that prefer to spend time with you alone rather than joining you two as a pair.

It might be enjoyable and a change of pace to spend time with friends without your husband, but it's crucial to be aware of the possible risk it poses to your marriage.

Many of us have friends who share our spouses' gender. We often bring old pals with us into new ones. However, since it raises the possibility of faithfulness and relationship dissatisfaction, this might possibly be harmful to your marriage. Even if you are guilt-free, your spouse may not like the time you spend with someone else. Trusting you to do what is right should be a component of marriage, but remember to balance or restrict the time you spend with others of the same gender as your partner out of respect for them.

Spending too much time with friends—especially those who are not part of the "our friends" group—can increase the chance of influence-related unhappiness. Even though having friends is vital for your personal development and evolution, it may also provide too many voices and ideas since the individuals you spend the most time with tend to have the greatest influence. This is particularly true when you and your spouse dispute on anything; it is only normal to seek counsel from friends in these circumstances. However, having too many friends and voices might be harmful to your marriage.

Although having close friends outside of your marriage might be dangerous, it can also be advantageous!

You may get a lot of mental peace from friends who share your beliefs, and this calm will help you treat your spouse with love and attention. Marriage is not always simple, but having a buddy or a couple to lean on may keep you both on track when things go tough. However, it is crucial to have wise and reliable friends who you can confide in and who you can rely to for sensible counsel.

Friendships may motivate one another. Just as they are for you, your husband and you may be an invaluable resource for another couple. Finding friends who share your ideals and outlook on life is crucial; those who disagree with your family's values are probably not the people you should look up to for inspiration.

As a pair, it's important to maintain relationships with others in your community. Without friendships, it is difficult to integrate into a group and experience others' support and encouragement. Family is a valuable resource, but they may not always be ready to give you the advice you need. But friends often provide the kind of stable support system that many couples need. Additionally, having connections might provide you and your partner the chance to help and encourage other couples in their life.

Even if you are aware that friendships outside of your marriage might be dangerous, you shouldn't let that stop you from asking for help. Instead, the advantages should provide you encouragement and a set of basic rules for developing closer relationships with others who will strengthen your marriage.

Made in the USA
Las Vegas, NV
20 July 2024

92514248R00037